D1377152

Famous Illustrated
Speeches & Documents

The Declaration of Independence

Stuart A. Kallen

Illustrated by Michael Birawer

Published by Abdo & Daughters, 4940 Viking Drive, Suite 622, Edina, Minnesota 55435.

Library bound edition distributed by Rockbottom Books, Pentagon Tower, P.O. Box 36036, Minneapolis, Minnesota 55435.

Printed in the United States.

Interior Photo credits: Bettmann

Edited by Julie Berg

Library of Congress Cataloging-in-Publication Data

Kallen, Stuart A., 1955-
    The Declaration of Independence / Stuart A. Kallen.
        p.   cm. -- (Famous illustrated speeches & documents)
    ISBN 1-56239-318-9
    1. United States.   Declaration of Independence--Juvenile literature.
    2. United States--Politics and government--1775–1783--Juvenile literature.
    I. Title.   II. Series.
    E221.K35   1994
    973.3'13--dc20   94-20198
                                           CIP
                                           AC

INTRODUCTION

Some people think that America began on the Fourth of July, 1776, when the Declaration of Independence was signed. But that's not exactly true. Native American people lived in America for thousands of years before colonists began to arrive from England in 1607. For the next 150 years, millions of people emmigrated from Europe to America. By 1776, over two million people lived in America's thirteen colonies. Most of their ancestors were from England.

England was the "mother country" of America. British lawmakers in England made the laws for Americans. British soldiers backed up those laws. And British tax collectors took money from Americans to support England. Americans were allowed to set up their own businesses, postal services, schools, and governments. After 150 years, many Americans were tired of British rule.

When England ran short of money in the 1770s, they raised taxes on Americans. When England put a stiff tax on tea, an American named Samuel Adams took action. Adams and his friends boarded British ships loaded with tea and dumped 342 tea chests worth $90,000 into Boston Harbor Massachusetts. This became known as the Boston Tea Party.

When word of Adams' Tea Party reached England, trouble began. Thousands of British soldiers were sent to Boston. They closed the harbor and would not let food and supplies into the city. When other colonies heard of this, they decided to support the people of Massachusetts.

Suddenly, all Americans had a common enemy — the British.

From Massachusetts to Georgia, trouble continued building between the American colonies and England. Americans banded together to fight. In April 1775, the first battle was fought between American and British soldiers in the Massachusetts towns of Lexington and Concord. War between "Mother Britain" and her American "children" had begun.

Some Americans were happy to be part of Britain. They only wanted the war to end, with England giving basic rights to the colonies. But men like Benjamin Franklin, Thomas Jefferson, and John Adams wanted to form a new nation with new ideas. As war raged on, Franklin, Jefferson, and 50 men gathered at the Continental Congress in Philadelphia, Pennsylvania, to plot a course for America.

The Continental Congress had representatives from all of America's 13 colonies. Some wanted independence, some did not. The Congress created a small committee to write a document to tell the world why America wanted to be free from England's rule. The document would be called the "Declaration of Independence."

John Adams formed the committee to write the declaration. The group also included Benjamin Franklin, Roger Sherman from Connecticut, a New Yorker named Robert Livingston, and a 33-year-old lawyer from Virginia, Thomas Jefferson. After much bickering, Jefferson said that he would write the declaration. No one else felt qualified to write such an important paper.

For the next two weeks, candles burned late in Jefferson's room. He wrote and rewrote the declaration. He searched his mind for every idea about how a government should be run.

Jefferson thought of new ideas that had never been tried. He felt that governments should not belong to kings. Governments should belong to the people.

On June 28, 1776, Jefferson laid down several tightly spaced pages of writing on the desk of the clerk of Congress. The new country of America had a written plan—the Declaration of Independence.

The declaration had three parts. The first part spelled out the reasons why America thought it had the right to be independent. The second part was a long list of evil deeds committed by the British. The third part stated that America was now a free and independent nation. It would break free of Britain and form its own place in the world. And Jefferson wrote that America would now be called "the United States of America."

Once the document was written, a debate raged in Congress over what it said. Some were afraid that America would lose the war with England. Then every man who signed the Declaration of Independence would be hanged for treason.

On July 2, 1776, the Continental Congress delegates voted to approve the Declaration of Independence. New York was not represented that day, but voted to approve the declaration several weeks later. It was done! The United States of America had been born.

Here are the words that Thomas Jefferson wrote in the first part of the Declaration of Independence:

When in the course of human events, it becomes necessary for
one people to dissolve the political bands, which have
connected them with another,

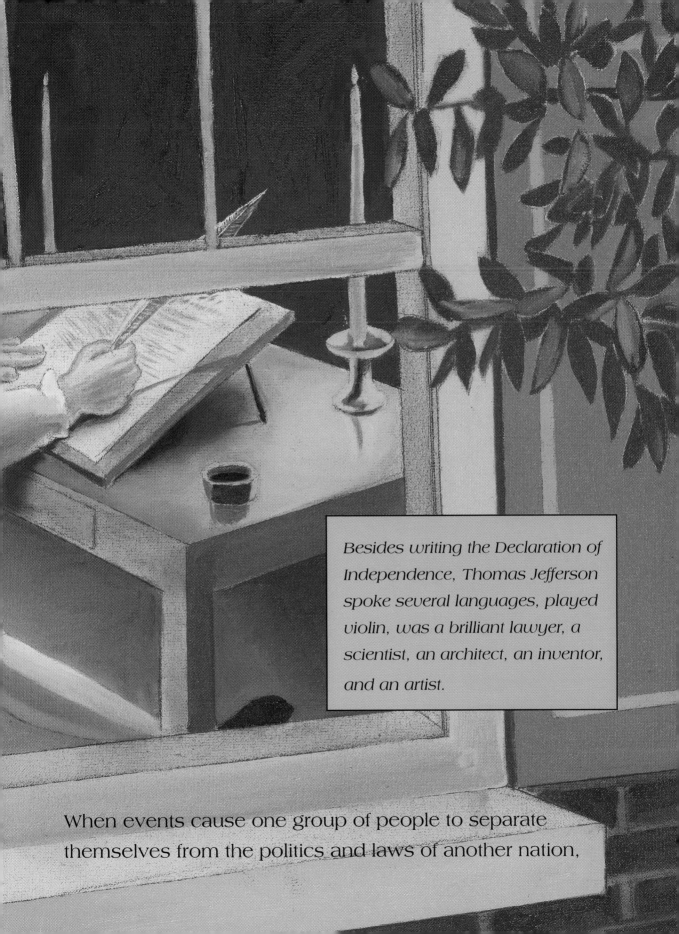

Besides writing the Declaration of Independence, Thomas Jefferson spoke several languages, played violin, was a brilliant lawyer, a scientist, an architect, an inventor, and an artist.

When events cause one group of people to separate themselves from the politics and laws of another nation,

Signing the Declaration of Independence

Atlantic Oce...

...and to assume among the powers of the earth, the separate and equal station to which the Laws of Nature and Nature's God entitle them,

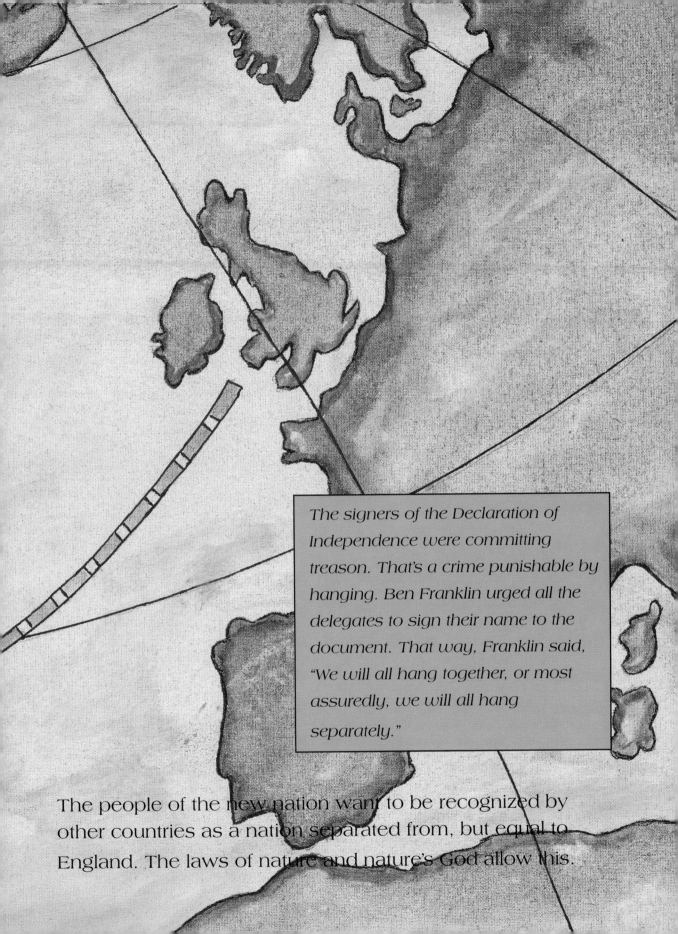

The signers of the Declaration of Independence were committing treason. That's a crime punishable by hanging. Ben Franklin urged all the delegates to sign their name to the document. That way, Franklin said, "We will all hang together, or most assuredly, we will all hang separately."

The people of the new nation want to be recognized by other countries as a nation separated from, but equal to England. The laws of nature and nature's God allow this.

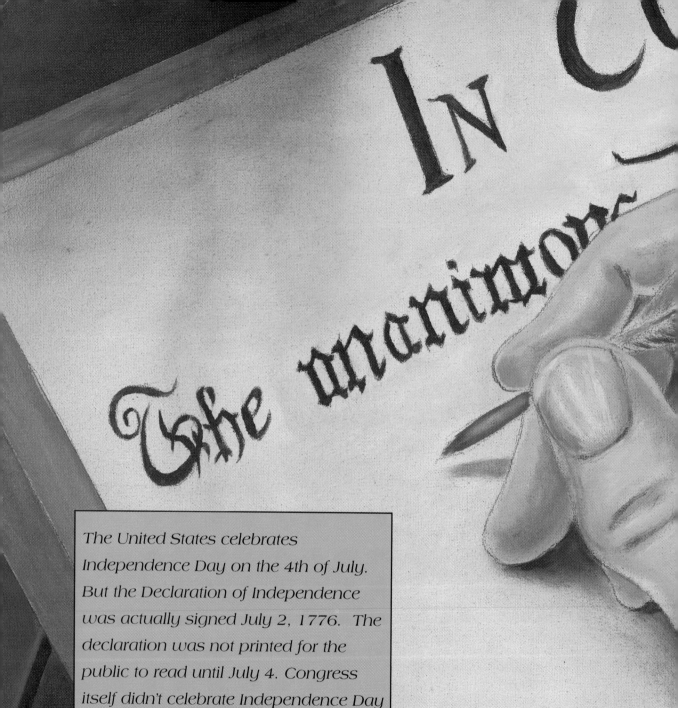

The United States celebrates Independence Day on the 4th of July. But the Declaration of Independence was actually signed July 2, 1776. The declaration was not printed for the public to read until July 4. Congress itself didn't celebrate Independence Day that year until July 8.

a decent respect to the opinions of mankind requires that they should declare the causes which impel them to the separation.

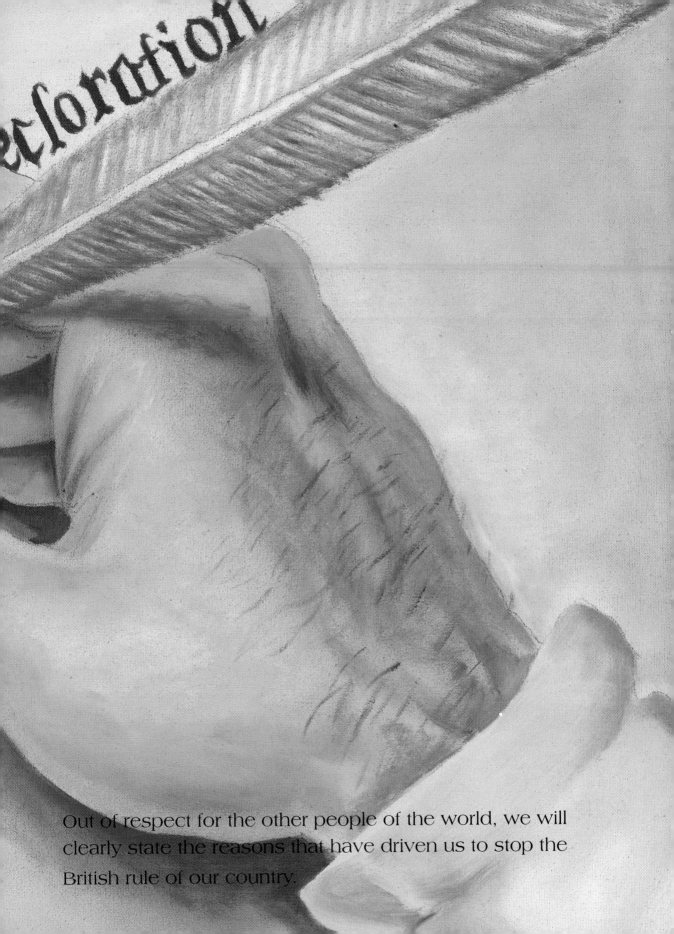

Out of respect for the other people of the world, we will clearly state the reasons that have driven us to stop the British rule of our country.

We hold these truths to be self-evident, that all men are created equal, that they are endowed by their Creator with certain unalienable Rights, that among these are Life, Liberty and the pursuit of Happiness.

When the Declaration of Independence was signed, half-a-million African-Americans were slaves. Jefferson wanted the declaration to also free the slaves. The colonies in the South refused to sign the document if it ended slavery. The words "ending slavery" were crossed out of the Declaration of Independence. Eighty-five years later, the Civil War would be fought to free the slaves.

This is the absolute truth that no one can deny—all people are created equal, they all have the right to life, freedom, and the chance to find happiness.

That to secure these rights, Governments are instituted among Men, deriving their powers from the consent of the governed,

By the time the Declaration of Independence was agreed upon by Congress, one third of Jefferson's original words had been changed.

Governments are formed to protect the rights of life, liberty, and happiness. But the governments must get their power from the people who are governed.

That whenever any Form of Government becomes destructive to these ends, it is the Right of the People to alter or to abolish it,

When Jefferson wrote the Declaration of Independence, his ideas were unheard of. Most people did not think everyone was created equal. Many thought that kings, queens, and nobles were born with special rights that no else could have.

When the government gets in the way of people's rights, the people have the power to change the government or do away with it completely.

and to institute new Government, laying its foundation on such principles and organizing its powers in such form,

John Adams, 2nd President
of the United States.

*Thomas Jefferson died on
July 4, 1827, exactly 50
years after the Declaration
of Independence was
published. John Adams
died the same day.*

When a government is bad, the people have a right to form a

es to them shall seem most likely to effect their Safety and

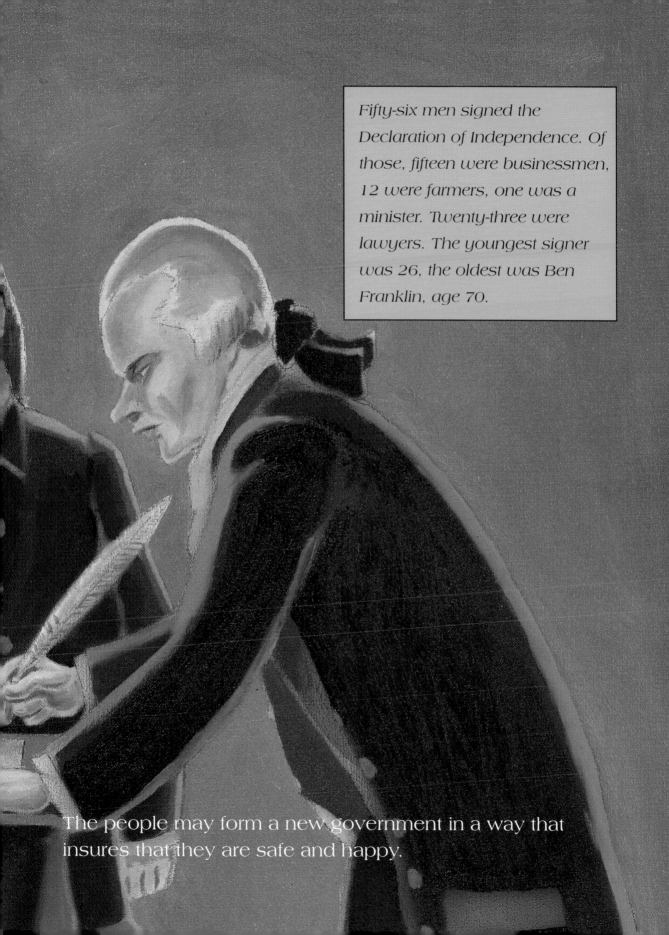

Fifty-six men signed the Declaration of Independence. Of those, fifteen were businessmen, 12 were farmers, one was a minister. Twenty-three were lawyers. The youngest signer was 26, the oldest was Ben Franklin, age 70.

The people may form a new government in a way that insures that they are safe and happy.

A FINAL WORD

On August 2, 1776, the Declaration of Independence was signed by fifty-six members of Congress in Independence Hall in Philadelphia. John Hancock was the first to sign. He wrote his name so large that "King George (of England) could read it without his spectacles."

Within days of being written, the Declaration of Independence was read to people far and wide. Crowds yelled and cheered when they heard Jefferson's inspiring words. When France heard that the United States had been formed, they began to ship money and supplies to the new nation. This helped America win the revolution against England.

After the signing of the document, it was simply rolled up and kept with other papers in Congress. Later in the war, when British soldiers closed in on Philadelphia, the declaration was tossed into a trunk and moved from city to city so it would be protected.

President George Washington took the Declaration of Independence to the new capital of the United States, Washington D.C., in 1789. There, the document remained in Thomas Jefferson's office. Jefferson was the Secretary of State at that time.

During the War of 1812, British troops burned the city of Washington. The Declaration of Independence was kept hidden in the home of a minister. After the war, someone tried to reproduce the document by sprinkling it with chemicals. This damaged it and caused many signatures to fade.

In 1841, the document was sandwiched between two pieces of glass and hung on the wall of the new U.S. Patent Office.

There it hung, exposed to light and fading for 35 years.

On July 4, 1876, the Declaration of Independence was taken to Philadelphia to celebrate the nation's 100th birthday. By then, much of the document was so yellow and cracked that it could barely be read.

In the 1920s, the United States built the National Archives to store important papers. A special exhibit was created for the Declaration of Independence. The case was sealed so that no air could further destroy the document. Special glass was made to keep light from destroying the writing. Each night, the document was safely locked away. Guards stood watch over the document. In case of emergency, the document could be lowered in seconds by a special elevator to a bombproof shelter. This is where the Declaration of Independence rests today.

The United States was formed using the Declaration of Independence as a plan. Over the centuries, dozens of other countries have used the declaration's words as a blueprint for their push for freedom. Even today, the United States still struggles to live up to the ideal put forth by Jefferson over 200 years ago. But using the ideas of life, liberty, and the pursuit of happiness, the road to freedom will roll on until everyone of us finds freedom.

The Declaration of Independence

In Congress, July 4, 1776

The unanimous Declaration of the thirteen united States of America,

When in the Course of human events, it becomes necessary for one people to dissolve the political bands which have connected them with another, and to assume among the powers of the earth, the separate and equal station to which the Laws of Nature and of Nature's God entitle them, a decent respect to the opinions of mankind requires that they should declare the causes which impel them to the separation.

We hold these truths to be self-evident, that all men are created equal, that they are endowed by their Creator with certain unalienable Rights, that among these are Life, Liberty and the pursuit of Happiness. That to secure these rights, Governments are instituted among Men, deriving their just powers from the consent of the governed, — That whenever any Form of Government becomes destructive of these ends, it is the Right of the People to alter or to abolish it, and to institute new Government, laying its foundation on such principles and organizing its power in such form, as to them shall seem most likely to effect their Safety and Happiness. Prudence, indeed will dictate that Governments long established should not be changed for light and transient causes; and accordingly all experience hath shewn, that mankind are more diposed to suffer, while evils are sufferable, than to right themselves by abolishing the forms to which they are accustomed.

But when a long train of abuses and usurpations, pursuing invariably the same Object evinces a design to reduce them under absolute Despotism, it is their right, it is their duty, to throw off such Government, and to provide new Guards for their future security. — Such has been the patient sufferance of these colonies; and such is now the necessity which constrains them to alter their former Systems of Government. The history of the present King of Great Britain is a history of repeated injuries and usurpations, all having in direct object the establishment of an absolute Tyranny of these States. To prove this, let Facts be submitted to a candid world.

He has refused his Assent to Laws, the most wholesome and necessary for the public good.

He has forbidden his Governors to pass Laws of immediate and pressing importance, unless suspended in their operation till his Assent should be obtained; and when so suspended, he has utterly neglected to attend to them.

He has refused to pass other Laws for the accommodation of large districts of people, unless those people would relinquish the right of Representation in the Legislature, a right inestimable to them and formidable to tyrants only.

He has called together legislative bodies at places unusual, uncomfortable, and distant from the depository of their public Records, for the sole purpose of fatiguing them into compliance with his measures.

He has dissolved Representative Houses repeatedly, for opposing with manly firmness his invasions on the rights of the people.

He has refused for a long time, after such dissolutions, to cause others to be elected; whereby the Legislative powers, incapable of Annihilation, have returned to the People at large for their exercise; the State remaining in the mean time exposed to all the dangers of invasion from without, and convulsions within.

He has endeavoured to prevent the population of these States; for that purpose obstructing the Laws for Naturalization of Foreigners; refusing to pass others to encourage their migrations hither, and raising the conditions of new Appropriations of Lands.

He has obstructed the Administration of Justice, by refusing his Assent to Laws for establishing Judiciary powers.

He has made Judges dependent on his Will alone, for the tenure of their offices, and the amount and payment of their salaries.

He has erected a multitude of New Offices, and sent hither swarms of Officers to harass our people, and eat out their substance.

He has kept among us, in times of peace, Standing Armies without the Consent of our legislatures.

He has affected to render the Military independent of and superior to the Civil power.

He has combined with others to subject us to a jurisdiction foreign to our constitution, and acknowledged by our laws; giving his Assent to their Acts of pretended Legislation:

For quartering large bodies of armed troops among us:

For protecting them, by a mock Trial, from punishment for any Murders which they should commit on the inhabitants of these States:

For cutting off our Trade with all parts of the world:

For imposing Taxes on us without our Consent:

For depriving us in many cases, of the benefits of Trial by Jury:

For transporting us beyond Seas to be tried for pretended offenses:

For abolishing the free System of English Laws in a neighbouring Province, establishing therein an Arbitrary government, and enlarging its Boundaries so as to render it at once an example and fit instrument for introducing the same absolute rule into these Colonies:

For taking away our Charters, abolishing our most valuable Laws, and altering fundamentally the Forms of our Gorvernments:

For suspending our own Legislatures, and declaring trhemselves invested with power to legislate for us in all cases whatsoever.

He has abdicated Government here, by declaring us out of his Protection and waging War against us.

He has plundered our seas, ravaged our Coasts, burnt our towns, and destroyed the lives of our people.

He is at this time transporting large Armies of foreign Mercenaries to compleat the works of death, desolation and tyranny, already begun with circumstances of Cruelty and perfidy scarcely paralleled in the most barbarous ages, and totally unworthy the Head of a civilized nation.

He has constrained our fellow Citizens taken Captive on the high Seas to bear Arms against their Country, to become the executioners of their friends and Brethren, or to fall themselves by their Hands.

He has excited domestic insurrections amongst us, and had endeavoured to bring on the inhabitants of our frontiers, the merciless Indian Savages, whose known rule of warfare is an undistinguished destruction of all ages, sexes and conditions.

In every stage of these Oppressions We have Petitioned for Redress in the most humble terms: Our repeated Petitions have been answered only by repeated injury. A Prince, whose character is thus marked by every act which may define a Tyrant, is unfit to be the ruler of a free people.

Nor have We been wanting in attentions to our British brethren. We have warned them from time to time of attempts by their legislature to extend an unwarrantable jursisdiction over us. We have reminded them of the circumstances of our emigration and settlement here.

We have appealed to their native justice and magnanimity, and we have conjured them by the ties of our common kindred to disavow these usurpations, which, would inevitably interrupt our connections and correspondence. They too have been deaf to the voice of justice and of consanguinity. We must, therefore, acquiesce in the necessity, which denounces our Separation, and hold them, as we hold the rest of mankind, Enemies in War, in Peace Friends.

We, therefore, the Representatives of the united States of America, in General Congress, Assembled, appealing to the Supreme Judge of the world for the rectitude of our intentions, do, in the Name, and by the Authority of the good People of these Colonies, solemnly publish and declare, That these United Colonies are, and of Right ought to be Free and Independent States; that they are Absolved from all Allegiance to the British Crown, and that all political connection between them and the State of Great Britain, is and ought to be totally dissolved; and that as Free and Independent States, they have full Power to levy War, conclude Peace, contract Alliances, establish Commerce, and to do all other Acts and Things which Independent States may of right do.

And for the support of this Declaration, with a firm reliance of the protection of Divine Providence, we mutually pledge to each other our Lives, our Fortunes and our sacred Honor.

GLOSSARY

Abolish - to put an end to.

"The 13 Colonies" - a group of thirteen states that were in America but under British rule of law. The thirteen colonies later became the United States of America.

Consent - to agree.

Declaration - a written or spoken statement that clearly announces something.

Deriving - obtaining or receiving.

Dissolve - to break up or put an end to.

Impel - to drive or urge forward.

Independence - freedom from the control of others.

Instituted - to have set up or started something.

Political - of or involved in government.

Pursuit - to gain or follow through with.

Self-evident - true, without argument.

Treason - committing crimes against one's own government. To overthrow one's government.

Unalienable - not able to be sold or transferred to another.